Trollerella

BY Karen M. Stegman-Bourgeois

ILLUSTRATED BY

Ethan Long

HOLIDAY HOUSE / New York

For my amazing dad, who taught me to persevere.
For my beautiful mom, who showed me how to find inner beauty.
For my incredible children, Justin, Josh,
and Stephanie, who keep me young.
And for my Prince Charming, Tom, who swept me off my feet
and still knows how to make me dizzy.
With love,

K. S.

For Fran Peacock Coker,
who loved children

E. L.

Text copyright © 2006 by Karen M. Stegman-Bourgeois
Illustrations copyright © 2006 by Ethan Long
All Rights Reserved
The text typeface is Olduvai Regular.
The art was created in pen and ink, then digitally scanned and colored.
Manufactured in China
www.holidayhouse.com
First Edition
1 3 5 7 9 10 8 6 4 2

Library of Congress Cataloging-in-Publication Data
Stegman-Bourgeois, Karen M.
Trollerella / by Karen M. Stegman-Bourgeois ; illustrated by Ethan Long.— 1st ed.
p. cm.
Summary: This version of the Cinderella story features
a troll living under a bridge who finds an invitation to a ball,
where she dances with Prince Charming.
ISBN-13: 978-0-8234-1918-0
ISBN-10: 0-8234-1918-5 (hardcover)
[1. Trolls—Fiction. 2. Fairy tales.] I. Long, Ethan, ill. II. Title.
PZ8.B64433Trol 2006
[E]—dc22
2005050332

LONG AGO, under a castle bridge, lived a troll named Trollerella. Every night she dreamed of being beautiful, but every day she woke up to the same gruesome reflection.

Trollerella's brother, Victroll, was proud of his ugliness and used it to his advantage. When a visitor approached the castle, he would make faces, hiss, and growl until the visitor threw him a gold coin. The bridge was soon called the trollway, and Victroll's fee was called the troll toll.

One day, after her morning cry, Trollerella heard the pounding of carriages on the bridge. She got there just in time to see an envelope fall to the ground.

"Wait!" she yelled. But the carriages were already gone.

Trollerella ripped open the lovely envelope and read: "You are cordially invited to the ball for the King's only son, Charlemagne, Prince Charming." Trollerella pressed her thin, slimy lips to the paper and sighed. "If only I could go to the ball."

"What'cha got there?" Victroll slithered from the sludge. Trollerella hid the invitation behind her back, but Victroll grabbed her arm and made her drop it.

"No!" She turned just in time to watch it drift into the well.

Victroll had a brief feeling of guilt, but it passed. "Probably a corny dance. I'll get plenty of gold tonight!" Then he slithered back into his troll hole.

Trollerella stomped away, or at least she tried to stomp.
In the mud, it was more of a slosh.

"I could have danced with the prince!" She pulled Victroll's
bag of gold from its hiding place, then pushed it into the
deep, dark well.

Suddenly there was a *POOF!*

"Hi diddly!" came a painfully shrill voice. A fairy flew out of the well, flitted a little as fairies do, and landed gently. "Hey doodly?"

"Um, hi," Trollerella returned the greeting. "Who are you?"

"I'm the tooth fairy. I live in this well." She was holding the invitation. "Oh! I see you don't brush. Tsk, tsk."

Trollerella smiled shyly.

"Well, well . . . get it? Well, well?" The tooth fairy laughed in delight. "I seem to have been invited to a ball."

"That invitation is mine," Trollerella explained. "My brother made me drop it."

"Oh." The tooth fairy twirled on one toe.

Trollerella asked, "Did you get the gold too?"

"Oh yes! Was that from you? Tell you what; to thank you for the gold, I'll give you anything you want."

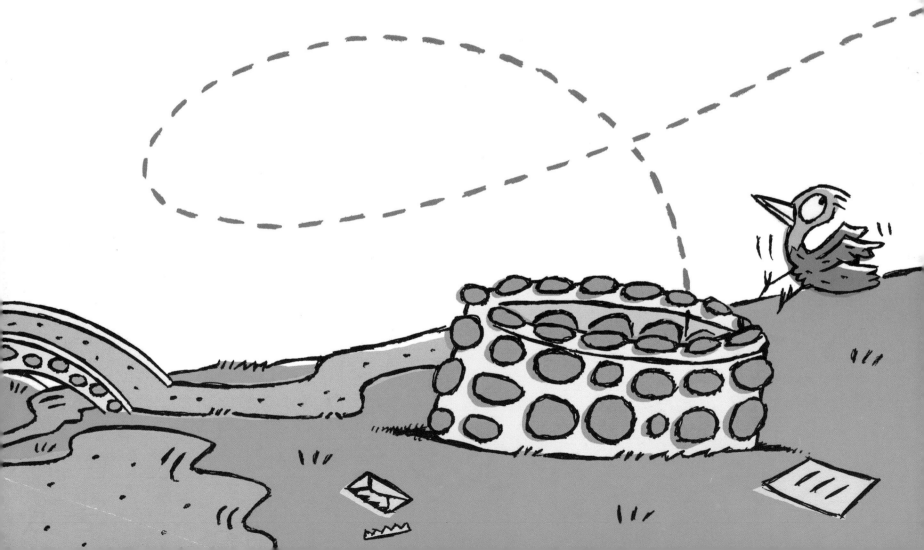

"Anything?"

"Yes. I'm a registered dentist, and I tinker with orthodontia. Perhaps you'd like a porcelain filling, braces, maybe a crown? A root canal? Bridgework?"

Trollerella looked at her bridge thoughtfully. It was already perfect.

"Could you make me beautiful for just one night?"

"Trollie, Trollie, Trollie. Ah! I have an idea. For one night only, everyone who sees you will *think* they see a beautiful maiden." And the tooth fairy waved her wand.

"Then I can go to the ball?" Trollerella beamed.

"Yessiree!" The tooth fairy tapped Trollerella on the head, and she became nearly clean. Another tap found Trollerella draped in a beautiful gown.

"Oops, almost forgot . . ." The tooth fairy tapped Trollerella's huge, slimy feet. Out of nowhere came two enormous, yet very fine, glass slippers.

"And, Trollie? Avoid cavity-causing sweets." Then, with another *POOF*, the fairy was gone.

By sundown the first carriage arrived. Victroll leaped into action, threatening the driver until he tossed the troll a gold coin. Trollerella decided she would be the last to the ball and make a glamorous entrance.

At ten o'clock Trollerella waited at the tooth fairy's well. When the next coach arrived, the coachman brought it to a screeching halt.

"My fine woman," he said, "please board my coach before the evil troll kidnaps you and hoards your beauty for himself."

Trollerella giggled, climbed on board, and tossed a coin to her brother.

The castle was elegant. Everything sparkled.

"May I get you a drink?" asked a handsome man.

Trollerella batted her eyelashes. "Do you have minnow water?"

He smiled a huge white smile and threw back his head, laughing. The tooth fairy would have loved this guy.

Everyone stared as the young man took Trollerella by the elbow and led her to the dance floor.

"You dance divinely," he said, spinning her like a top. "Can I get you something to drink now?"

"Do you have slug broth?"

The handsome prince laughed. "Oh, you kill me."

Trollerella panicked. "I would never! My brother might, but I . . ." She didn't feel right. She thought she might be sick. She had to escape.

Across the room, a lovely woman was being escorted from a pumpkin carriage. As all eyes turned to her, Trollerella ran. She looked back only once to see her prince dancing with the new girl.

When she got home, Trollerella realized that she had lost one of her lovely glass slippers. She cried until a commotion on the bridge brought her back to her senses. The clock was chiming midnight, and there, running from the castle, was the young woman from the pumpkin carriage.

She too seemed to be having trouble keeping her glass slippers on. One of them fell off onto Trollerella's very own bridge, but Trollerella decided to leave it there in case the girl returned for it.

The next morning, Sir Reginald left the castle with Trollerella's glass slipper on a pillow.

"Send a proclamation. All eligible girls will try on this slipper. Whomever it fits will marry the prince."

Trollerella couldn't believe her ears. She went to the well. "Hello!" she called. "Hi diddly. Hey doodly!"

POOF! The tooth fairy emerged. "Hi diddly yourself, Trollie. How was the ball?"

"Wonderful! But I got nervous and dropped a shoe and the prince found it and now he wants to marry me!"

The tooth fairy danced. "This could be a dilemma. This wand doesn't have enough power to make you seem beautiful forever."

"No?" Trollerella felt tears pooling in her great big eyes.

"Now let Toothy think." She rested her chin on the wand. "Yes, I have it. I'll just make the prince fall in love with you. But you must promise to brush and floss regularly."

"I promise!"

"Feather of ostrich, tail of a dove, Trollie gets Prince Charming's love. Done!"

By the end of the day, the shoe and the king's men were on their way back to the castle. They were downhearted, having not found the girl. Trollerella stopped them at the bridge.

"No troll tolls, please," Sir Reginald said. "We've had a bad day."
"I want to try on the slipper," Trollerella said shyly.
"You?" Sir Reginald asked, then began to chuckle.

The others followed, laughing louder and louder until Trollerella grabbed the shoe and put it on her foot. "There! See?"

The laughter stopped. "The shoe fits the troll!" Sir Reginald yelled.

Trollerella was carried to the castle on the pillow with the shoe. The trumpeter sounded the arrival of the bride-to-be, while the prince sat on his throne and waited impatiently.

Everyone was silent.

The prince stood and walked to Trollerella. "You blundering idiots!"

"We're sorry," Sir Reginald explained. "We didn't find anyone who fit the shoe. This troll made us stop. She wanted a toll, but, but, but..."

"Stop babbling." He took Trollerella by the hand. "My bride has not been given the engagement ring."

"Oh, sorry." Sir Reginald reached into his pocket, pulled out a tiny ring, and gave it to Trollerella.

"Put it on me?" Trollerella asked the prince.

"Certainly." He tried to pry the ring onto her long, bony finger, but it wouldn't fit. Then he noticed a large wart on her nose. He gracefully set the ring on the wart and kissed her.

Everyone in the room felt his or her stomach turn but smiled and applauded. Trollerella was to be the new princess.

Meanwhile outside, under the bridge, Victroll was happily playing with his newest find, the shiny glass slipper from the small woman in the pumpkin carriage. He could hear the sound of the moat water in it.

And in a small house in town, Cinderella was packing her bag. She'd had enough abuse from her stepmother and stepsisters. She was going to move to the big city and start her own cleaning business.

And you already knew that Trollerella and Prince Charming would live happily ever after.